Snakes on the Hunt

VIPERS

Dava Pressberg

PowerKiDS press

New York

Published in 2017 by The Rosen Publishing Group, Inc.
29 East 21st Street, New York, NY 10010

Copyright © 2017 by The Rosen Publishing Group, Inc.

First Edition

Editor: Caitie McAneney
Book Design: Mickey Harmon

Photo Credits: Cover, pp. 1, 4, 6, 8, 12, 16, 18 (series logo) iLoveCoffeeDesign/Shutterstock.com; cover, pp. 1, 3, 4, 6, 8, 10, 12, 14, 16, 18, 20, 22—24 (background) cla78/Shutterstock.com; cover (viper) Willie Davis/Shutterstock.com, p. 5 (rattlesnake) Amee Cross/Shutterstock.com; p. 5 (cottonmouth) Jason Patrick Ross/Shutterstock.com; p. 5 (copperhead) Ryan M. Bolton/Shutterstock.com; p. 7 (horned viper) https://commons.wikimedia.org/wiki/File:Hornviper_Cerastes_cerastes.jpg; pp. 7 (diamondback, copperhead), 13 Dennis W. Donohue/Shutterstock.com; p. 9 John Cancalosi/National Geographic Magazines/Getty Images; p. 11 jo Crebbin/Shutterstock.com; p. 15 (inset) Andre Coetzer/Shutterstock.com; pp. 15 (main), 21 (inset) reptiles4all/Shutterstock.com; p. 17 Paul S. Wolf/Shutterstock.com; p. 19 Jiri Herout/Shutterstock.com; p. 21 (main) Matteo photos/Shutterstock.com; p. 22 Ging o_o/Shutterstock.com.

Cataloging-in-Publication Data

Names: Pressberg, Dava.
Title: Vipers / Dava Pressberg.
Description: New York : PowerKids Press, 2017. | Series: Snakes on the hunt | Includes index.
Identifiers: ISBN 9781499422108 (pbk.) | ISBN 9781499422122 (library bound) | ISBN 9781499422115 (6 pack)
Subjects: LCSH: Viperidae-Juvenile literature. | Poisonous snakes-Juvenile literature.
Classification: LCC QL666.069 P725 2017 | DDC 597.96'3-d23

Manufactured in the United States of America

CPSIA Compliance Information: Batch #BS16PK: For Further Information contact Rosen Publishing, New York, New York at 1-800-237-9932

Contents

A Deadly Bite

What slithers on the ground and has a bite that can kill? It's the **venomous** viper! These snakes use a deadly poison to **disable** their **prey**.

Vipers are any members of the snake family Viperidae. This big family is made up of more than 200 species, or kinds, of snakes. Some snake specialists break Viperidae into the smaller groups of pit vipers and Old World vipers. Pit vipers have a heat-sensing **organ**, while Old World vipers don't. Rattlesnakes, copperheads, and cottonmouths are all pit vipers.

Snake Bites

Old World vipers are part of the subfamily Viperinae. They're also called true vipers or pitless vipers.

cottonmouth

copperhead

rattlesnake

Vipers are a wide-ranging family. They're all quite different from each other, but they're all venomous!

Viper Bodies

There are many species of vipers, and they come in many sizes. The longest pit vipers in the world are bushmasters. They can grow to more than 10 feet (3 m) long! Other vipers are only a few inches long.

Viper species come in many colors and patterns. The western diamondback rattlesnake is often gray and green with a diamond pattern. Copperheads are tan and rust-colored. Most vipers, including cottonmouths, rattlesnakes, and horned vipers, have triangle-shaped heads.

Snake Bites

One of the smallest vipers in the world is the Namaqua dwarf adder. It only grows to about 11 inches long (28 cm)!

copperhead

diamondback
rattlesnake

You can **identify** this horned viper
by the two horns on its head.

A Viper's Life

Most vipers are solitary animals, which means they prefer to live and hunt alone. However, some, such as rattlesnakes, will share a den from time to time. Vipers do have to come together to mate, or make babies.

Most snakes lay eggs. However, most pit vipers give birth to live young. That means the mother viper doesn't lay eggs. She carries eggs inside her body, but her babies break out of the eggs before they're born. Many Old World vipers also give birth to live young. However, some species lay eggs.

Snake Bites

The bushmaster viper is the only pit viper that lays eggs instead of giving birth to live young.

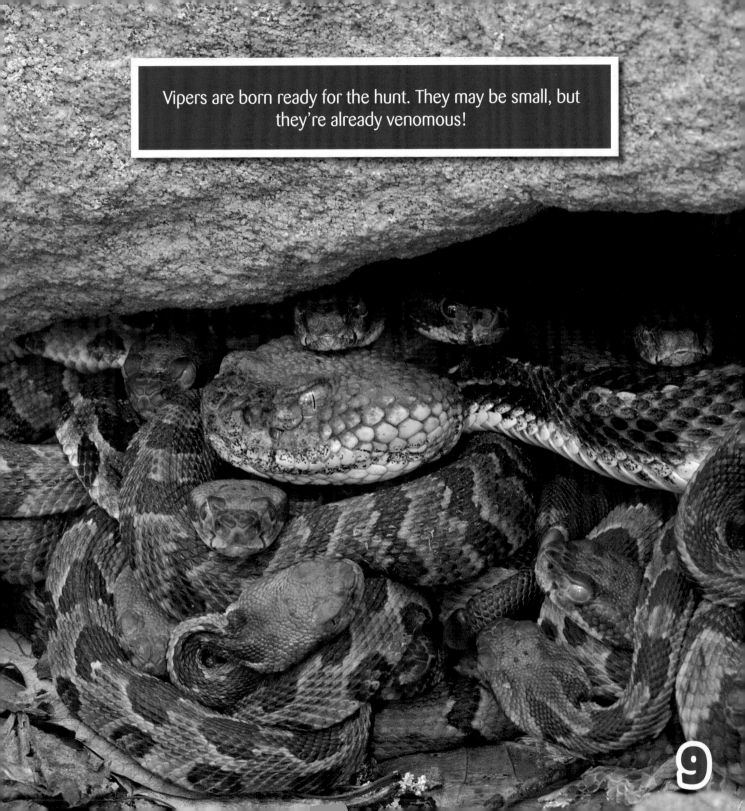

Vipers are born ready for the hunt. They may be small, but they're already venomous!

9

Viper Habitats

Vipers are found all around the world. They live in **regions** of North America and South America. Other vipers are found in Europe, Asia, and Africa.

Vipers live in many different **habitats**. Some, such as the western diamondback rattlesnake, live in the deserts of the U.S. Southwest and Mexico. The bushmaster viper lives near the Amazon River. Many vipers may be found in trees. Others may be found slithering and building dens along the ground. Some vipers, such as the cottonmouth, spend a lot of time in water.

It's important to know which venomous snakes are found in your region. The cottonmouth snake lives in the southeastern United States.

11

Amazing Senses

Snakes have amazing senses that help them hunt. It might sound funny, but snakes smell with their tongue. They stick their tongue out to pick up a smell. Then they pass the tongue over a special body part called the Jacobson's organ. It's located at the top of their mouth, and it can recognize smells.

Pit vipers have a really cool supersense. They can sense heat from other nearby animals using their pit organs. The pit organs are located between their eyes and nose.

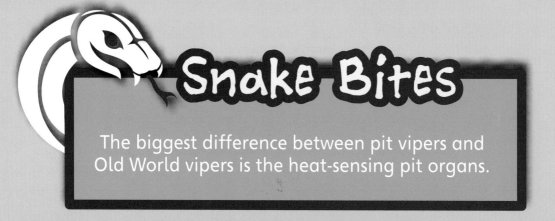

Snake Bites

The biggest difference between pit vipers and Old World vipers is the heat-sensing pit organs.

nostril

pit organ

Pit organs help a pit viper track down its prey after it bites.

Using Venom

Not all venomous snakes are vipers, but all vipers are venomous. These snakes are feared around the world because of their deadly bite.

A viper delivers its venomous bite with its fangs. These fangs are curved, hollow teeth. They're sharp enough to break the skin of prey and then **inject** their deadly poison. When a snake isn't biting, the fangs fold up inside its mouth. Some scientists believe adult vipers can control the amount of venom they want to use. They know how much it'll take to disable their prey.

Some vipers are more deadly than others. One of the most venomous vipers in the world is the saw-scaled viper found in the Middle East and central Asia.

viper fangs

saw-scaled viper

A Viper's Diet

Different species of vipers hunt different kinds of prey. That's because they live in different regions of the world.

Many vipers eat whatever they can find, catch, and fit down their throat. They can stretch their jaws wide to swallow big meals. They often hunt small **mammals** found in their habitat, such as rats and rabbits. Some also catch birds, lizards, and frogs. Vipers that swim, such as cottonmouths, may feed on fish, small alligators, and turtles.

Snake Bites

Because vipers eat small animals, they help control those **populations**. That makes them important to their **ecosystem**.

This cottonmouth is eating a bullfrog.

Venomous Hunter

Some snakes called constrictors squeeze their prey to death. Vipers, on the other hand, don't always hold on to their prey.

Vipers are known to strike with a bite that disables the prey first. If the prey runs away, it quickly loses strength and often dies. A pit viper can track the prey using its heat-sensing organs. It opens its mouth wide and swallows the prey. Like most snakes, vipers don't have to eat for a while after a big meal.

Snake Bites

Young cottonmouths and copperheads have an interesting hunting skill. They flick the tip of their tail back and forth so it looks like a worm. That's **bait** for small frogs and fish!

Most vipers hunt at night. They use their supersenses to find prey in the dark.

Vipers in Trouble

When animals are in danger of dying out, they're said to be endangered. Some animals aren't completely endangered, but their population is getting smaller.

Many viper species are at risk. One big reason is habitat **destruction**. People cut down trees and build on land that used to be vipers' homes. Some vipers are killed for their skin, or their venom is used in medicine. Some vipers are critically, or seriously, endangered, including the Wagner's viper and the Orlov's viper.

In 2013, nine Wagner's vipers were born at the St. Louis Zoo. People used to think this species had died out completely.

Orlov's viper

Wagner's viper

From a Distance

Vipers are amazing hunters. They use their supersenses to track down prey, even in the dark. Then they strike with a deadly bite. There are many different species of vipers, and each one plays an important part in its ecosystem.

How can you help vipers? Tell people about their great skills and features, and the dangers they face from habitat destruction. Don't buy products made with snakeskin. If you see a viper, let it go on its way. You can enjoy it from a distance!

Glossary

bait: Something that's used to attract fish or other animals so they can be caught.

destruction: The state of being ruined.

disable: To make something incapable of moving or working in its usual way.

ecosystem: All the living things in an area.

habitat: The natural place where an animal or plant lives.

identify: To tell what something is.

inject: To force something into the body using a needle or sharp teeth.

mammal: A warm-blooded animal that has a backbone and hair, breathes air, and feeds milk to its young.

organ: A body part that does a certain task.

population: The number of animals in a species that live in a place.

prey: An animal hunted by other animals for food.

region: A large area of land that has a number of features in common.

venomous: Having a poisonous bite.

Index

Websites

Due to the changing nature of Internet links, PowerKids Press has developed an online list of websites related to the subject of this book. This site is updated regularly. Please use this link to access the list: www.powerkidslinks.com/soth/viper